MONICA
SELES

*(Photo on
front cover.)*

**Fourth-round
action in the
1992 Wimbledon
Championships.**

*(Photo on
previous pages.)*

**Seles wins her
third Virginia
Slims
Championship in
a row.**

Text copyright © 1997 by The Child's World, Inc.
All rights reserved. No part of this book may be reproduced
or utilized in any form or by any means without written
permission from the Publisher.
Printed in the United States of America.

Photography supplied by Wide World Photos Inc.

Library of Congress Cataloging-in-Publication Data
Rambeck, Richard.
Monica Seles / Richard Rambeck
p. cm.
Summary: Relates the story of the Yugoslavian-born
tennis player who made a comeback after being stabbed in 1993.
ISBN 1-56766-312-5 (hard cover library bound)

1. Seles, Monica, 1973 -   -- Juvenile literature. 2. Tennis
players --Yugoslavia --Biography--Juvenile literature.
3. Women tennis players --Yugoslavia --Biography --
Juvenile literature.
[1. Seles, Monica, 1973-   . 2. Tennis players. 3. Women --
Biography.]
I. Title
GV994.S45R35   1996   96-14171
796.342'092 — dc20   CIP
[B]   AC

MONICA
SELES

BY RICHARD RAMBECK

Seles makes a
return in a
warm-up
session with
her brother.

Monica Seles was where she had been many times before. She had just won the Australian Open, for the fourth time in her career, and was about to get the championship trophy. Seles looked around the tennis stadium in Melbourne where the Open was held. She loved playing here. She loved playing in this tournament. And why not? She had never lost a match in the Australian Open. After winning the 1996 tournament, she was 28-0 in the Open.

When Seles was handed the trophy, her eyes filled with tears as the fans cheered her. "It's just great to be back," Seles said, her voice starting to break. "I still can't believe I'm here." For a while—for nearly two years—it had seemed as though Seles might never play top-level tennis again. After winning the 1993 Australian Open, she didn't play for nine weeks because of a bad case of the flu. Her next tournament was in Hamburg, Germany. It would be her last competition for 28 months.

Seles wins the 1990 French Open.

In the quarterfinals against Maggie Maleeva, Seles was resting on the sidelines between points when it happened: a man with a knife came out of the stands and stabbed her in the back. At first, Seles didn't even know she was hurt. As it turned out, though; the knife wound was serious. Her life wasn't in danger, but her tennis career was. It all seemed so cruel.

Seles was the top-ranked woman player in the world. And she was only 19 years old.

Monica Seles won her first Grand Slam tournament at age 16 when she captured the 1990 French Open title. (The Grand Slam is made up of four tournaments—the Australian Open, the French Open, the All-England Championships at Wimbledon, and the U.S. Open.) In 1991, Seles not only won the French Open again, she was also the top finisher at the Australian and U.S. Opens. In 1992, she played in the finals of all four Grand Slam events. She won three, losing only to Steffi Graf in the Wimbledon final. Seles became the top-ranked women's player in the world in 1991, and was the youngest woman ever to earn that honor. The tall left-hander—she's five feet 101/2 inches tall—simply overpowered almost all of her opponents. Only Graf, who had been Number 1 in the world for several years until Seles came along, had the game to stay with Monica. Seles was so successful because she never stopped playing as hard as she could. She put all her effort into every shot.

Before she was stabbed in April 1993, Seles had played in the finals of the last nine Grand Slam events she entered. She had won seven of those tournaments. After the stabbing, though, she could

Seles grimaces as she makes a return against Ruxandra Dragomir.

barely raise her left arm above her head. There was more than pain for her to overcome, however. She had constant nightmares about the attack. What if she did start playing in big tournaments again? she wondered. Could it happen again? Suddenly, fear had become Monica Seles' strongest opponent.

For more than two years, Seles spent most of her time at her home in Sarasota, Florida. (Although she was born in Yugoslavia, Seles and her family moved to the United States to live when she was 12.) At home, she played tennis with her father, Karolj. This was fun for Monica. Tennis with her father was like a hobby—something to do to fill the day. "When my dad and I finish practice, we never take tennis off the court," she said. "We're able to go back to being father and daughter."

S eles, however, knew she also wanted to go back to being a professional tennis player. By the summer of 1995, she believed she was ready to return to the game. She entered the Canadian Open. She didn't expect to win; she merely wanted to play. "You just do your best," Seles said before the tournament. "That's all you can do. It's going to take a while [to be able to play the way she used to]. If it doesn't take a while, that's great." At the Canadian Open, Seles played as if she had never been away.

Seles makes a return in the 1995 U.S. Open.

Monica Seles won the 1995 Canadian Open title with ease. In five matches, she lost only 14 games and not a single set. She beat Amanda Coetzer 6-0, 6-1 in the final. It was an easy ride to a championship for Seles. The next tournament, however, would be much more of a test. She entered the U.S. Open for the first time since 1992. In the first round, she beat Ruxandra Dragomir 6-3, 6-1. "It's very good for women's tennis that she's come back, but it was bad for me," Dragomir said after the match.

Seles kept winning until she reached the final against Steffi Graf. It was a battle of the world's two top players, and Seles had played in only two tournaments in the last two and a half years. Graf won the first set 8-6. Then Seles took the second 6-0. It was the first time Graf had ever lost a set on a Grand Slam event by a 6-0 score. Graf, however, came back to win the third and final set 6-3. Graf claimed the championship, but there was no doubt that Seles was back.

Seles, left, hugs Steffi Graf after the final match in the 1995 U.S. Open.

Seles, though, didn't play any more tournaments in 1995. She had problems with her knee, ankle, and left shoulder. Then she had a few dizzy spells. Before the 1996 Australian Open, Seles won another tournament in Australia. Despite the victory, she didn't feel right when the Australian Open began. Her

injuries had left her a little out of shape. German star Boris Becker said Seles "was really miserable" when the Australian Open began. "But," Becker added, "she is a tough cookie."

Despite her aches and pains, Seles made it to the final. She almost lost in the semifinals to Chanda Rubin. Rubin, in fact, could have taken a big lead in the third set, but Seles fought back and won. "If you don't take charge, she will," Rubin said. Seles then defeated Anke Huber 6-4, 6-1 in the final. After the match, Seles thought about the last three years. "I almost felt like it was '93," she said. No, it wasn't 1993, but Monica Seles was definitely back and on top of her game.